A Thousand Paths to Friendship

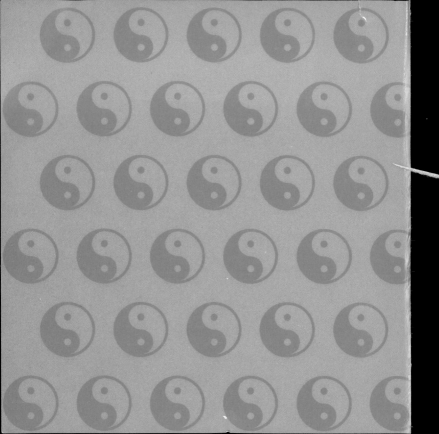

A Thousand Paths to
friendship

David Baird

MQP

Contents

Introduction

Friendship is the greatest single feeling mankind can experience and the greatest gift we can give to another person. With it we become stronger and more creative; more caring toward ourselves and toward others, and much more humane.

This wonderful, beautiful, diverse world we share can also be a fearful and fretful place. We have all lived through some form of crisis, terror, or war which has left its mark on us whether at first hand or via media coverage. So now, more than ever perhaps, the world is in need of friendship to replace the "eye for an eye" attitude that blots out the sun. Friendship begins within ourselves and those closest to us, but from these modest roots it is capable of stretching out to the four corners of the globe and enriching the lives of everyone in this world.

Here within these pages, my friends, we shall explore the gift of friendship in all its beautiful guises. Let's start making friends today and begin a journey that will scatter the seeds of this inspirational bond to all our new friends and neighbors around the world.

Bosom
Buddies

Friendship is like love, only with no strings attached.

Our friends not only know all about us, but they take the huge leap of loving us despite it.

Life is filled with people who will wish you luck for their own sake, your true friend will wish you luck for your own sake.

Nothing can sweeten the soul more effectively than friendship.

Our friends are those around us who are closest to the most intimate aspects of our lives.

Faithful friends are worth more than money—they remain when the money runs out.

Friendship is love that comes with a lifetime guarantee.

Friendship is a tree to take shelter from the storm, to find shade from the blazing sun, to climb its branches to get a better view, and to swing from when we're happy.

Our friends in this lifetime are our guardian angels heaven sent.

It is a wonderful thing to see friendship in action and experience two friends each intent on promoting the good and happiness of the other.

Friendship that withstands the test of time sees many things around it wither. But in each other's eyes friends only become lovelier over time.

The only place you may be completely stupid and enjoy getting away with it is in the company of your best friend. Anywhere else would be fatal to your character or relationship.

The best gift anyone could ever give to themselves is the gift of a friend.

There is no greater thing two friends can do for each other than simply to be each other's friends.

True friendship survives time and distance and provides us with a feeling of oneness that is everlasting.

These days anyone can be reached by all manner of means: e-mail, text messaging, telephone. Friends can always be reached—even if we have to call collect.

A true friend
can be trusted
with your life
and your wallet.

There is no safer feeling than the comfort of sheltering from life's storms in the harbor of friendship.

What better way is there of proving that we believe in someone than to entrust them with our friendship and our hearts?

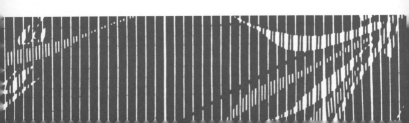

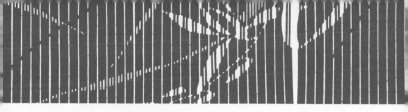

A day spent in the company of a close friend is like a mini vacation or a cause for celebration.

True friends are there for us unconditionally, offering us their support regardless of the circumstances.

When everybody else says go, your friend will tell you to stay.

A good friend
and companion
is one who
is willing to
sacrifice
everything for
the sake of
the other.

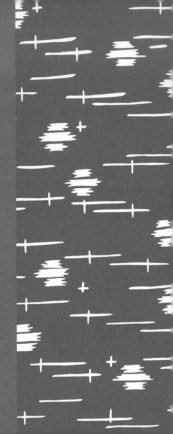

People tend to hear what they want to hear—a true friend always knows what it was that you meant to say.

To destroy a friendship the mutual respect each friend holds for the other must be damaged beyond repair.

Nothing inspires quite so much as the spiritual inspiration that comes from discovering that someone wishes to be our friend.

Friendship is the shortest distance between two hearts.

Only a fool would sacrifice the happiness of friendship.

Hold a true friend with all your might.

If you truly want to know someone, ask their friend.

When a close friendship is formed with another it is as if there were one mind in two bodies.

We go through life alone thinking we are the only one who feels a certain way about things, and then suddenly someone comes along who feels exactly the same way. It's the start of a beautiful friendship.

By offering our hand to another in friendship we also offer our heart. And a great deal of our life.

Friendship grants many wishes.

Friends do not count up each other's faults, and neither do they keep each other waiting.

Anyone can be in two places at one time when they have a friend.

Side by
side each
step of
the way

Regardless
of all
obstacles

This is the
journey of
friendship.

Regardless of how slight their acquaintance, those who have grown old together seem bosom buddies.

Like good wine, where the friendship is the oldest there is the greatest trust.

Perhaps the time to begin thinking about coloring your hair or having a facelift is when your best friend begins commenting on how young you look.

Life is to be fortified by many friendships. To love and to be loved is the greatest happiness of existence.

Sydney Smith

The cutest quirk of friendship is perhaps the way friends always seem to believe themselves wiser than you in whatever it is they may say or advise.

Your friend will sing out your praises,
Yield to your superior abilities,
Applaud your wisdom,
And ignore your advice.

A best friend overlooks your failings and tolerates your successes.

Pets are good friends—they ask little of us, never pass judgement on us, and are not critical of the way we are.

Friendship is the warmest, most comforting bosom in which to bury one's head in times of sorrow.

Friends bring humor into our lives— that keeps us going.

Friends cherish the silences that they share together, as though that which is not said is as essential somehow as that which is said.

With a close friend one feels twice the courage and life doesn't seem quite so hard.

Sometimes life can be petrifying— one becomes fearful of looking forward or backward. That is when we realize that if we look beside us, our friend is there.

The arrival into our life of a true friend when our inner spirit feels all but burned out, rekindles even the minutest ember to burst once more to the full flame of life.

We can get through life without humor, without courage, without wealth, and even without love. But a life without friendship would be impossible.

Friends pick us up when we fall, and if they cannot, they lie down beside us and listen for a while.

There is only a short step between friendship and brotherhood.

Friends will always find a feast, even where there are only onions and water.

When you reach out your hand through the fog of doubt or the darkness of your torment, the person who is there to take hold of it is undoubtedly your friend.

A lifelong friendship is a perfect reason for having a clear conscience.

You may know anyone by the company they choose to keep.

The road to a friend's house is never long.

The unspoken bond of friendship translates as: "If you should ever need my life, then come and take it."

Best friends will rarely, if ever, tell one another that they are best friends. It is simply a fact known to them both.

Good company in a journey makes the way too seem the shorter.
Izaak Walton

Chance made us friends, but with time we may become as close as siblings.

True friends stick together through all the inclement elements, rather like the ivy on the old rectory wall.

Praise your friends, and watch them blossom.

After a lifetime of friendship that has crossed the slopes of despair, trodden trails paved with tears, seen anger, fear, and dismay, ask two friends what they remember and they will say laughter and the good times they shared.

A friendship built upon one seeking power over the other is destined to fail. When two friends find influence and inspiration from each other, that friendship will last for ever.

In the company of friends we are free to be as mad as March hares.

Make hay while the sunshine of friendship is upon you.

When two friends work together they make light of any task.

A friend will not only give you his lamb, but also his sheep.

One cannot guarantee having a single good friend simply because one has accumulated a great many friends.

More grows in the fields of friendship than either friend will ever sow.

Two friends may be close, but just because one hurts their foot, the other should not be expected to limp.

We accept our friends as they are and as they offer their friendship to us—they are gift horses, and to check out their teeth would be an insult.

Some get confused between friendship and shadows—our shadow is the thing that does everything we do as we do it. The value of a friend is that they don't nod when we nod, or change just because we change.

The most satisfactory form of intoxication comes not through wine but from being in the company of friends.

Friends will go out of their way to do good turns for each other.

The chemistry of friendship is like any other reaction—both are transformed and something new is created.

A good friend always makes the season.

Two people meet and something inside each is fueled by an intense response to the other. Each probably think they are the only one to feel that way, until suddenly it becomes clear to both that a friendship has just been born.

When two friends have willing hearts, nothing is impossible to them.

Anyone who has a friend has faith, hope, and charity in their life.

One flower may not make a garland, but a single friend will make a garden.

With a
single
friend

We live
two lives

With two
friends

We live
three lives

And so it
goes on.

You know you are friends when you not only sit at each other's table, but also feel comfortable enough to put your feet up on it.

Friends know that to ease each others heartaches is also to forget one's own.

The only time a friend will mention another friend's debts is when they offer to pay them.

True friends have the strength of character to acknowledge each other's stronger and weaker points while remaining in perfect harmony.

The wonderful paradox of friendship, of two being as one, magnifies the soul for all to see.

Friends are alike in many ways. And also very different.

A true friend will not wait to carve what they think of you on your tombstone—they'll tell you while you are still capable of blushing.

To each of us, our friends are the very best of humankind.

When a friendship is close, words become irrelevant.

The path that leads to your friend's house can only be kept clear of weeds by the journeys you make along it.

Laughter is the flagship of friendship—wherever there are two people laughing and sharing, you will discover a sweet spring of friendship.

Each of us has a huge array of complex and varied moods. The miracle of friendship is that we are blessed with someone else who is capable of understanding them, or is at least prepared to try!

The person who goes through life feeling boredom must be friendless, for when we have friends boredom is not an option.

Friendship provides us with feelings of safety and comfort.

Our friends take us as we are—
The rough with the smooth
The chaff with the grain
The sweet and the sour.

Always strive to be a bit better than your best friends imagine you to be.

A friend is the icing on life's cake.

No person should ever be made to feel inferior to their own best friend.

If you wish to reap friendship sow courtesy—he who plants loving kindness, harvests loving friends.

Friendship is a path that runs parallel to our own destiny. Friends meet there and travel side by side in the same direction, sharing each other's burdens and enjoying each other's company— never abandoning each other or their own journey.

There is silence. And there is silence that is shared with a friend. They are quite different, and to be missed when they are no more.

Are you single? Not if you have a friend, for friendship is a marriage of two minds, two hearts, and two souls.

Our friends don't need to say hurtful things about us behind our back—they'll air their grievance face to face.

Life without
friendship would
be like waking
to darkness
every morning.

Friendship is a single soul that resides in two bodies.

Life is a great stealer of time, and friendship requires as much as we can give it. Respect your friends and celebrate friendships with time spent in their good company.

When the bond of friendship is forged between two people, the unseen, unspoken contract is that truth exists between them forever.

Beautiful
friendship
is found
where
self-interest
is not.

Friends are our partners in the dance of life, not to be dropped when the ball ends.

The fire in the hearth burns warmer in the presence of two friends.

If you go into friendship go with all your heart.

Remember before burdening others that even our very best friends have their own fears, loves, and losses to contend with.

How rare and wonderful is that flash of a moment when we realize we have discovered a friend.

William E. Rothschild

Friendship is pure distilled love.

Friendship exists to be seen: hide it from the world and it is as a secret forest where no one will ever see the blooms or smell the sweet scents, but share it with the world and all can enjoy its beauty and help it grow.

Let the crystal waters of friendship wash over you and cleanse away all the baneful vexations of life.

To live a great life, one leaves it knowing one has had good friends.

Friendship is about being at ease with someone special—when our mind is at ease our spirit is at peace.

We go through each and every day making new acquaintances, but we're lucky if we go through life with one true friend.

Our friends are the garden in which we plant our trust, our hope, our love, and our faith and in which we give thanks for each blossom.

My best friend is not only my best friend—my best friend is my second self.

Friendship is the dwelling place of the divine: there is no fame or profit here, only the deepest joy of two spirits at peace. How tranquil it is!

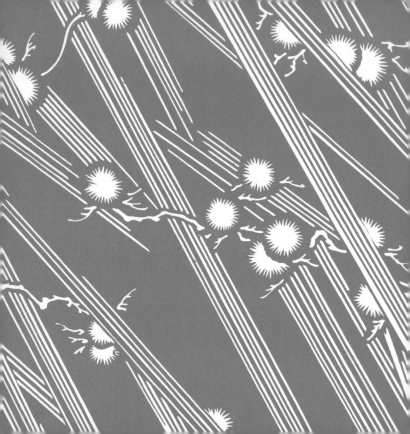

The Art of
Friendship

The only way to have a friend is to become one.

Friends are merely people like you and I.

All of us should allow ourselves one gift in life and that is the gift of friendship.

Somewhere out there is someone who was born to be your friend.

Somewhere out there is someone who was born for you to be their friend.

It is not difficult to take the first step to eternal friendship. All it takes is something two people have in common, say, a dislike of anchovies.

The secret to developing
a good friendship is to
develop the art of being
a good listener.

When friendships are new and uncertain, they are like new season citrus fruits—one may ripen into the sweetest of oranges, another may become a bitter lemon.

A true friendship is always easier to find than a true and lasting love.

The house of friendship should be kept in a constant state of repair.

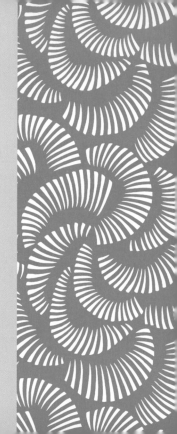

We call it a
circle of friends
because a circle
is never ending.

**Nature's most
wonderful
masterpiece
is friendship.**

Friendship is like a precious pearl that forms over time from the minutest speck into a rare jewel of immense beauty and value that all admire and envy.

A friend is like a hard-cooked egg—each has a heart of gold.

Friendship is a work of art, and should always be displayed in the best light possible.

Friends are like good books—well chosen, relatively few, always cherished, and regularly revisited.

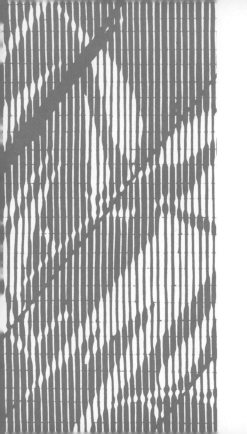

Spiritual
friendship
rattles us
out of our
unawareness.
It creates an
opening to
horizons
never before
contemplated.

Our greatest glories are measured in our friends.

By day and by night all spirits wake and shine in the radiance of friendship.

If I had to trust in one power in life it would have to be the power of friendship.

Friendship is a vast horizon always expanding, always inspiring.

What would this world be if no person had the courage to attempt friendship?

Friendship is about the greatest jewel a person can have. It outshines diamonds and can cut through anything.

Many set out seeking friendship, but waste their lives searching for perfection.

Friendship that is not for the sake of our own self-interest is very rare indeed and of great beauty when it is found.

You cannot go to the market and buy yourself a friendship, it is a homemade recipe.

A life of ease is not such a difficult pursuit when we have friends.

Friends are kind to each other's dreams.

Friendship planted in the garden of our hearts will grow despite any heavy frost of adversity.

How can anyone contemplate developing friendships if they can't bring themselves to be their own friend?

A friend is someone who knows the song in your heart, and can sing it back to you when you have forgotten the words.

There should be no rush in choosing a friend. And even less so in changing one.

Each of us must define for ourselves the qualities that make a friend, for who could possibly hold all the elements essential to meet with everyone's concept of a true friend?

Why use a thousand words
when you can use just one?
The word *friend* says it all.

**When you are blessed
with friends, they are
your true estate.**

The easiest way to tell
what a person is, is by
the company they keep.

The meaning attached to each friendship is without words, without language.

Remember, all but your friends will judge you by your actions, not your intentions.

If you wander through life looking for friendship with your eyes, you will miss it. Friendship is seen with the heart.

Friendship is the orchard in which friends grow. If you are unable to appreciate the apple then the orchard will be meaningless to you.

Friendship is not a means to an end.
It is both the means and the end.

The more sorrow one encounters in a lifetime, the more joy one's friendships contain.

Friendship has no frontiers—everybody feels good and laughs in the same language.

Some say the best friend to have is an egotist. They won't talk about you behind your back when they could be talking about themselves.

Friendship makes us near perfect.

Friendship is in the details.

There is no time like the present to become friends.

Friendship is the very best of medicines.

True friendship lasts forever and everyone wants it, but few understand that to get a true friend one must become a true friend.

Friendship
is a single
tree under
which many
can enjoy
the shade.

Many a marriage is cemented together by the bond of mutual friends.

Friendship is an invitation to afternoon tea.

Friendship reflects our very best self.

Listen to your friends.

Our friends are to be accepted as they are and we should never try to change them. One can dress a big loveable hairy ape in satin, but it will still be a big loveable hairy ape.

The two things that make a lifetime into something glorious are friendship and learning.

If there is one formula for friendship it is this: meet it as a friend.

Friendship must be actively sought—if you just wait for friendship to arrive "one of these days," that day may never come.

Deep down, we feel
unworthy of true friendship.

It's not something you learn in
school. But if you haven't learned
the meaning of friendship, you
really haven't learned anything.

Muhammad Ali

Choosing a friend is like choosing a favorite book. Some offer adventure and enlightenment, while others have the potential to bore you to death.

We must all confront the fear we feel when we risk working at friendship.

There is nothing to compare with having friendship in our lives.

Life is filled
with dares,
but friendship
dares us to be
ourselves.
Therefore,
make your
first friend *you*.

Never leave friendship to chance. That would be like promising yourself a trip to Paris and depending upon getting there by sleepwalking.

Your own good cheer is important, for it is friendly to the mind and to the body.

We should all take great pains to protect our personal integrity, for without it how can we ever be confident enough to seek out friendship?

Friends should provide for each other mutual sympathy and always seek to supply what the other lacks.

Love your friends for their sake rather than your own.

A handful of rice will suffice for a meal, but a handful of friendship will feed you for a lifetime.

Friends are like watermelons, you can't hold two in one hand.

What is friendship?
It is trust, empathy,
confidence, love,
faith, and mercy.

Friends will give each other the impression that they seek to be equals, but their friendship really survives because both have ambition beyond that.

When you have friendship you always have something of worth.

If you want one year of prosperity, grow grain.
If you want ten years of prosperity, grow fruit trees.
If you want a lifetime of prosperity, grow friends.

Friendship is like strong black coffee—stimulating.

Friendship is not necessary to life, but it does increase its value a thousand fold.

True friendship starts by getting to the bottom of yesterday's problems.

Claude Arpi

Two friends lay in the grass
Soaking up the sunshine.
It's good to grow old
Content together.

Sometimes it takes the arrival of friendship in our lives to show us who we really are.

Friendship liberates us. It makes us free to love.

The nicest present anyone can give themselves is a friend.

Friends
care and
always
will care.

Friendship is not
taught. It thinks
for itself.

The very best
way of being is
to find happiness
in friendship.

**Friendship is a form of recognition
of another's resemblance to us.**

Friendship is so beautiful
it can only be touched
with your heart.

**Friendship is the universal
obtainable treasure, often
obscured by our dreams of
silver and gold.**

Friendship has us taking less than we need and giving more than we can afford.

For friendship to enter the room the door must first be open.

Friendliness uplifts humanity.
It offers great dignity and its
importance in the affairs of
humankind should not be
underestimated.

**From the seeds of a new friendship
sown come an entire new world.**

He who gets close to a friend
will have a good friend.

Just living our lives leaves little time for anything else, but time dedicated to our friends will be rewarded seven fold.

With a friend by your side even a stroll through the park can become a daring adventure of discovery.

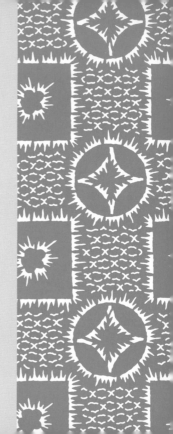

Two memories are better than one.

Show me your friends and I will tell you who you are.

Sometimes people come into your life and you know right away that they were meant to be there.

Good times are even better when they're shared.

Two things are everlasting—memories and friendship.

When you have a friend you have someone in your life who will take you just as you are.

No friendship is truly given that is not done so unconditionally.

Our friends are there to help us, and we are there to help them.

Friends can raise our spirits, even when the darkest cloud looms overhead.

Friends will always give encouragement: they are God's way of taking care of us.

A friend is someone who comes into your life and you feel as if they have always been around.

Ask a friend for water and they'll try to give you an ocean.

Ask a friend for directions and they'll accompany you all the way to your destination.

Do not enter into friendship with any great expectations, except the expectation of what you intend to give.

Friends
will give
each other
the best
years of
their lives,
and try to
protect
each other
from the
worst.

You will always live in interesting times when you live for friendship.

By bringing out the best in our friends we find we bring out the best in ourselves.

With friendship in our lives there is always something special to live for.

The important thing for one friend is to know what is important for the other.

No person is a true friend
unless they desire for their
friend that which they desire
for themselves.

**Our friends are the stars
that glow in the darkness.**

**Friendship should always
be answered with honesty.**

Always have faith
in your friend.

**A friend's welcome
never ends.**

**Serve your friendship
with no trace of ego.**

Love is friendship.
Live in that.

**Friendship belongs to all.
It is universal.**

When we need to hear the truth about ourselves, it is always best heard from our friends.

Do not seek to follow your friend's path, you will end up walking like him. Follow your own path, it runs alongside.

There is no greater statement of hope and faith than being someone's friend.

Some of us wait a long time for a real friend to come along.

Friendship does not just fall into our laps—it takes time to nurture patience and commitment. This is important, for once we have friendship, it is difficult to wriggle out of it.

Many a good friendship is made along the way through life—each is a stepping stone to happiness.

What is it that unites the hearts and minds of people? Friendship.

When one friend falls
The other is there to help.
If both should stumble
They shall help each other.

For Better or
For Worse

Our friends know all of our vulnerabilities and weaknesses.

Your truest friend, when they see you as you really are, will never run away.

Friends stick together, bringing comfort at times of terror, depression, and pain.

Friends don't avoid trouble—they develop a capacity to handle it.

Friends stand beside each other through thick and thin.

Friend, I am your friend, but
never shall I be your possession.

**Friends cherish
each other's hopes.**

A friend is someone who understands
our doubts and uncertainties and
sees our worth beyond them.

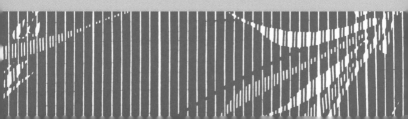

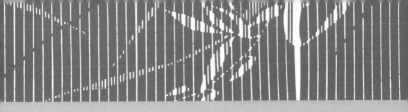

In times of prosperity friends will be plenty; in times of adversity not one in twenty.

English Proverb

It is said that the love and affection of a friend in a lifetime is that of a thousand mothers.

Friends should hold onto each other with both hands, that way neither can sling mud.

When your friend goes momentarily off the rails, remember that, even the best good egg may be slightly cracked.

Beware of suspicion—it is the cancer of any friendship.

The friendship that survives is the one that continues after the fighting and beyond the arguments.

We take our friends into our lives, their quirks and flaws and all.

Friendship gives and forgives.

Genuine friendship includes the willingness, for our friend's sake, to volunteer ourselves for activities which are not rewarding to us.

Friendship is something we offer even when those we offer it to are unable to acknowledge our help or show any gratitude.

Genuine friendship involves a genuine concern for others.

People will often sacrifice things of great importance to themselves for the sake of a friend.

Friends will never make assumptions about us, neither should we make assumptions about them.

Friendship sometimes means accepting situations which, on the face of them, hold nothing for you.

Never avoid a friend who is in need.

No person is poor when they have friends.

Each of our friends are a shelter for us, as we are for them.

A friend is a friend regardless of their circumstances. Be faithful to them when they are in need and know they will act in the same way toward you.

Hate me for who I am rather than love me for who I am not.

If you enter into friendship knowing there will be times when you are going to hurt and be hurt, you can apologize and forgive each other in advance.

Don't give up your friends—it will take a lifetime to forget them.

Friends are never afraid to tell each other just how they feel.

Give each friend the attention they deserve.

Do not allow any friend to overpower you.

The anxiety of one friend cannot be resolved by the anxiety of the other.

Sometimes we must allow ourselves to become emotionally detached from our friendships, so we can help our friends objectively.

Everyone will support a person when they believe them to be in the right, but only a true friend will stick by you even though you may be in the wrong.

It is not friendship if we cannot stand to see our friends succeed where we have failed.

In business we are loved for our merits, our friends love us for our faults.

Encouragement from my friends helps me feel strong enough to face life's hardships.

Our moments of unhappiness will show us where our true friendships lie.

Friendship is the freedom to express ourselves to another, never having to weigh our thoughts, never having to measure our words.

Friendships last that are careful to avoid those things in life that are unforgivable.

Pain is a momentary gap between two moments of friendship.

We all have moments in our lives when we cease to believe in ourselves, but when we have friends, they believe in us no matter what.

Friendship is, after all, another kind of marriage and is just as liable to divorce.

Some people give you a headache, friends will give you heartache after heartache.

Be prepared: friendship is infinitely more demanding than love.

When all the noses around you go up in the air, the one on the reassuring face of your friend remains parallel with your own.

Who would not prefer a friendly refusal to unwilling consent?

Self-love can cloud our judgment,
which is why it is always good to
consult our friends on things that have
the potential to reflect badly upon us.

**What greater anguish
than that for a friend?**

A friend will unhesitatingly help
with deeds at times when
deeds are called for and
words alone are meaningless.

Friendship is the acid test that affirms our fundamental worth.

When your heart has been broken, a friend will teach you to trust again.

Our friends are not mind readers. Why, even a baby must cry before her mother offers her milk.

A friend is a friend regardless of material standing. Just because our friend is not wealthy, that does not make the friendship defective—even the most expensive things on earth can be lacking in quality.

Do not be greedy of your friends: eat and drink of their goodwill but never gorge yourself on it.

Don't look upon friendship as an opportunity. Consider it more as a wonderful responsibility.

Never try to talk your friend into something they would rather not be involved in. It would be like giving them your best silver knife to stab themselves in the heart with.

There is no better provider of friendship than shared adversity.

Friendship is a marriage of minds.

Friendship is one of the most vital aspects of life.

It is not so much our friends' help that helps us as the confident knowledge that they will help us.

Epicurus

We must all accept that we will suffer to some degree throughout our lives, but when we have a good friend we need never suffer in solitude.

Whenever your faith is in doubt consider your closest friend and your faith will soon be restored.

Friendships, like any relationships, have their difficulties, but like a pair of shoes, only the wearer knows where they rub.

Our truest friend will still be there for us even when they are faced by the reality of their own powerlessness to change our situation.

Good friends are like parachutes—they catch us and gently bring us back to earth when we are in freefall.

When the chips are down it is good to realize that when you have friends you really do matter to someone.

Friendship is the best poultice for all wounds.

The joy of friendship can scatter a thousand griefs.

Friendship isn't a hobby, it's a full-time occupation.

No one dries tears quicker than a friend.

When a friend suffers misfortune, do not wait for an invitation to comfort and support them.

Friendship is an elaborate feast that must be delicately prepared before it can be enjoyed.

Friendship knows when it's best to keep both eyes open and when to turn a blind eye.

Who will show you love even during times of trouble? Your friends: they will be there for you in good times and in bad.

If you can bring yourself to honor a friend who has prospered without envying them, your friendship will have wonderful character and can survive anything.

Friends somehow get past the things that bother us about ourselves, and manage to like us anyway.

Friends will go out of their way to forgive each other.

Friends make the transition between birth and death far less troublesome than it would otherwise be.

When friend washes friend both are cleansed.

A friend listens just as intently to what you don't say.

Friends should set examples for each other. If we wish to improve our friend we must first improve ourselves.

Seek the good in others and they will seek the good in you.

One should treat the friendship with one's own children as sacred, and not chastise them for something we would let go with a good friend.

Friends who can forgive each other's little failings will remain friends for life.

A friend, when the situation calls for it, can always be relied upon to remember a thing or two that never transpired.

He who sows courtesy, shall reap friendship.

At the very mention of a friend's name an image of them forms in our minds and we feel instantly inspired.

Friends understand when we need to be alone, but a best friend also knows exactly when to come back.

Where there is friendship there is infinite possibility.

In our heart our friends
voices whisper to us.
We must find stillness
and give ourselves
pause to listen.

Plant your friendship
good and deep so
that it cannot be
uprooted.

Each friend is a bridge between ourselves and the real world.

Friends are created to be useful to each other.

Friends are like angels— they help our spirits fly.

Friends may forget the words we said, but never how they made them feel.

Friendship requires, at the very least, an interest in people for their own sake, and a willingness to put their interests before our own.

The world is filled with suffering, with friends we never have to worry about suffering alone.

Friends are not ashamed to seek out each other's shoulders to cry on.

Before entering into friendship, ask yourself if, in the long run, it will be worth your blood, your wealth, your sweat, and your tears.

As friends we enjoy each other on a platform of equality, while love thrives on opposites and extremes.

The miracle of friendship is that each seems to instinctively recognize what makes the other happy.

True friendship has forgiveness at its foundation.

Friendship is where the hearts are open and forgiving and acceptance is the rule.

The process by which people become friends involves not only talking to them at great length, but also listening to them.

No friend has ever been hurt by anything they didn't say.

We are faced with two choices: to ask a friend's forgiveness, or to reverse the treatment of the friends we wrong.

Friendship has its cloudier moments too, but friends know that all sunshine and no rain makes a desert.

A friend is someone we can trust with our most secret thoughts.

Friends provide us with equilibrium.

A friend will always forgive an unintentional mistake.

My friends have made the story of my life. In a thousand ways they have turned my limitations into beautiful privileges, and enabled me to walk serene and happy in the shadow cast by my deprivation.

Helen Keller

Be sensitive to the fact that some good deeds may backfire by imposing upon our friends a debt of gratitude they may not wish to acknowledge.

For friendship to work, friends must appear to each other only as they really are.

Friendship has great resources for it consists of two hearts.

True friendship can never be broken, weakened, or strained; it can only be tested.

Friends have no need to thank us, for what we do comes from our hearts.

Forgive your friends their little vices for these are illnesses of the soul cured only by example, not sermons.

Friendship brings sunshine and darkness into our lives. The darker moments are there so that we might occasionally see the stars.

Partings

No friendship can survive if you enter into it already wondering how it's going to end.

Pity those whose friendships have long been forgotten.

Fair-weather friends are like footprints left in the sand— washed away with the tide.

Distrust friendship that only reveals itself in the tents of prosperity. Real friendship is out there in the withered field.

Let all friendship begin with laughter and end, if it must, with a smile.

Friendships fail because the closer we become to another person, the more disagreeable we tend to become. Lasting friendship demands lasting courtesy, understanding, and great tact.

Life without friendship in it is an empty castle built on the sand.

You will never realize what you have until the moment comes to say good-bye. In that instant everything you took for granted will be revealed.

Losing friends is like losing your hair—friendship lost rarely grows back.

One can get through life without many things, but a life without friendship would be unbearable.

Each person is the sum of all their friends. Remove these and they stand alone and incomplete.

What is life without friendship?
It is like the heavens without the stars,
the sky without the sun.

**It is often said that
friendship can end in
love, but that love never
ends in friendship.**

There is one thing in life that is impossible to forget. And that is a lost friend.

Why is there no word to describe the loss of a dear friend? In life we can become widowed or orphaned, but the loss of a true friend leaves us speechless.

No friend would have us lament their passing, but would prefer us to celebrate the fullness of their friendship.

Even on the most cloud-filled night we know that the stars are still out there. And so it is with those friends, who we are not always able to see.

Everyone has some experience of losing friends.

Which will come to us first— tomorrow or our next life? Who can tell?

Let me lose my money,
My place in line,
My hair, my teeth,
And even my direction,
But please, oh please,
May I never lose my friends
For that would be to lose
   everything.

Experience tells us that we may lose people along the way, but we will never lose the mark they made upon our lives.

Sometimes in order to find friendship, change is involved. Become a friend to change, and change may bless you with the friendship you seek.

To lose any friend is hardship enough, but to forget them would be as if a part of you had died.

Don't wait until your friend is leaving to discover just how special they are to you.

With the sweet memory of a friend carried in our hearts, we can reunite through simple meditation.

Grief is a friend;
It serves to remind us,
It makes us take action,
It is our teacher,
And our foothold back to joy.

The first voices we will hear after this world will surely be those of the friends who went ahead of us.

Our greatest glory will be ending our allotted time on earth, not with accumulated wealth and riches, but with friendship intact.

Some of the tiniest things known to mankind are acts of friendship. Only the receiver can know how much a postcard, telephone call, or message from a friend can mean.

One should handle friendship like all fragile things in life— with great care.

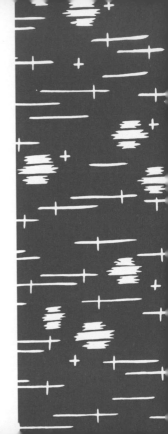

Friendship demands no physical pleasure, power, material profit, constancy, or oath of duty. It is without deceit.

There is no wilderness like life without friends; friendship multiplies blessings and minimizes misfortunes; it is a unique remedy against adversity and it soothes the soul.

Baltasar

Those who go through life fearing a broken heart will never know what it is to love a friend.

It is easier to stay out of friendship than to get out of it once you are in it.

Go often to the house of a friend; for weeds soon choke up the unused path.

Proverb

The light of old friendships may
    burn dim
But in the pitch dark of our
    blackest moments
The flicker from their candle
Is as the lighthouse beacon that
    saves the ship
From devastation on the rocks.

A true friend will feel free to speak the truth, and will not feel compelled to leave immediately afterward.

Just as each rose has its thorn, every friend has a friendly rival.

Every gastronome at some time seeks out the comfort of junk food. The worst discovery for any friend, would be to find out they were just somebody's frankfurter!

A true friend will always be on hand to help you move—even if you want to move mountains.

Some people get frightened of friendship and consider it too big for them to handle.

We do not have to go out and find a soul mate before it is possible for us to have the transforming power of friendship in our lives.

Occasionally it is good to come to regard a painful experience as an old friend. Sit with it a while and you will come to know it, to understand it, and to no longer wish to push it aside or pretend it doesn't exist.

You can always recognize a friend: they'll be the one that walks toward you when all the others walk away.

A friend to everybody is really a friend to nobody.

The best medicine in life is to have several dedicated faithful friends.

Friendship is a little bit like your finances—both are easier to make than they are to keep, and take work to do so.

No single person will ever possibly be able to combine all the essential elements each of us believes makes for the perfect friend.

One should serve one's friend for the love of doing so and not to win favor in the hereafter.

Friendship is friendship, but accounts must be kept.

We should all learn the value of friendship before, not after, it is lost.

Time passes.
If we are to be friends then we
    must be friends now,
Or return one day to the place
    where we were children
And discover that when we call
    out our friend's names
Their answer no longer comes,
Only our echo.

Friendship is the art of not only saying the right thing to a friend at precisely the right moment, but knowing when to leave things unsaid.

Wherever they may be in the world, good friends travel together in each other's hearts.

Friendship is incompatible with pity.

Never put off until tomorrow the friendship that can be begun today.

If you are going to bank on your friendship, then you must occasionally make a few deposits.

Friendship involves growth as we become more intimate and reach new levels of individuality and confidence.

Friendship is walking into a room filled with thousands of strangers and spotting your friend in an instant.

A friendship divided against itself will tumble.

Feed friendship on praise alone and it will starve.

No friendship that has been real can ever cease.

Friendship is quick to forgive and to forget.

All friendships benefit from each partner spending some time alone.

Friendship must never be paid for at the cost of everything else in your life.

**One cannot pen up friendship—
it requires freedom and fresh air.**

Even sickness, poverty, or
disgrace will not be able to
shake true friendships.

Friendship is the greatest pleasure we may hope for: and where we find it not at home, we seek it abroad.

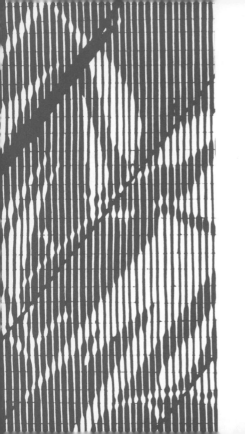

A person
can be
measured
by counting
the rings of
friendship
formed
through
their
lifetime.

Protect your friends from your actions as they will inevitably feel half guilty for all your misdeeds.

A vessel may be filled over a lifetime
Drop by precious drop
Or swiftly filled with a sudden gush
And emptied twice as quickly.

Some people collect friends much the same way as children collect empty seashells.

The important thing is to be virtuous enough not to be tempted away from friendship by self-love.

The vain are more worried about the end of their youthful looks than the death of their friendship.

Help and friendship go together, but no friend should continually ask for help.

Friendship may be bitter at times, but its fruit is always sweet.

Discretion is a pillar of friendship.

Get friendly: if all humankind were so
horrible, then God would stop
sending babies into the world.

**Talking about friendliness is not as
effective as being friendly.**

Until you can become friends with yourself, you'll never be content with the friends that surround you.

I have no talent for making new friends but, oh, such genius for fidelity to old ones.

Daphne du Maurier

We all hurt our friends from time to time, and they hurt us too. But friendship is forgiving by nature and will survive all storms.

Do not calculate the length of time you have spent in the company of your friend. Instead, consider how much time you have wasted away from them.

Nothing is as burdensome as a secret kept from a friend.

Friends should always part tenderly in case they may never meet again.

Do not let your desires tarnish the surface of your friendship.

Friendship waits outside like the sun's rays. It takes us to open the door for its light to flood into our life.

Our distance from friendship is the same as the distance from ourselves.

Hardship deepens the roots of true friendship.

For a person's divine nature to manifest itself through friendship they must sacrifice their ego, cease thinking of "mine," and begin a life of "ours."

Friendship survives not only by pruning its branches but also by tending to its roots.

Let differences between you and your friends exist and flourish. Respect them as long as they do not extinguish the flame of unity.

True friends leave a lasting impression on your heart.

It is better not to begin a friendship out of gratitude; these are shallow roots which are easily pulled out.

True friendship is to understand and to be understood.

Friendship is eternal—it has no birth or death.

Don't wait until friendship has been lost to realize how valuable it is.

Like two trees in an orchard, friends grow separately, yet never grow apart.

**We have all lost friends;
We have left friends behind,
They have abandoned us,
We have let them down.**

We enter life with nothing more than hope and promise—and exit carrying the memories of our friends.

A World
Shared

Pity those who go through life believing that we are born alone, that we live alone, and that we die alone. With love and friendship in our life we are never alone.

When you need them most, your friends are there for you. They'll never let you down.

Friendship is two people enjoying each others company in the comfort of silence.

When two people become close friends, joy is doubled in the lives of them both and they both have their grief divided.

Friendship
improves
happiness.

**Friendship
is a union of
two spirits.**

Are you ever single when you have a friend?

With a friend one is able to celebrate just being alive.

One of the most special forms that love can take is the love of friendship.

Friendship is about shared activities and self-disclosure.

Friendship is a kindly smile, an outstretched hand, the joy of companionship.

Everyone needs someone with whom they can share their secrets.

Friends that laugh together and cry together don't necessarily need to jump into the flames together.

What are friends for if not to share the good times and the bad?

Friends take out equal shares in each other's toils and troubles.

The greatest gift we can possibly give to another is a portion of ourselves.

One can wrestle with one's enemy, or find something that you can both laugh about. Find the common ground and you can share the path to a friendlier future.

Life need never be burdensome if you share the load.

With each new friendship a new world is born.

Have you ever wondered what the world would seem to us if we still lived at a time before we had our friends?

This world becomes a paradise when we have friends to share it with.

There is an entirely different world that only friends share—together they have a unique way of looking at, and experiencing, life.

Without friendship we are alone in this world—tiny floating islands drifting aimlessly between our limitations and our true potential.

Our friends walk in when the rest of the world walks out on us.

No matter how much distrust there is in this world, trust this: you will always be able to find someone to be your loving friend.

The world is round—
humankind should strive to
encircle it with friendship.

The true estates we build and leave behind us on earth are our friends and the effects of our friendship on the world we shared.

When two people decide to be friends they are making a statement to the world that they are connected to one another.

The world feels far from inhabited when we wander it alone.

One cannot just have friendship for oneself— it is designed to be shared, and that's why we have been given it.

We share many smiles and many tears with our friends, but nothing is better than the laughter.

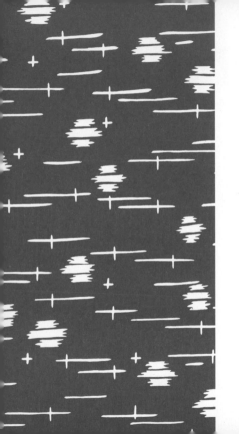

Why should two people go two different ways to the same place when they could go together?

Friends lead by example,
not through explanation.

Shared joys make a friend...
Nietzsche

The world's salvation is
located in friendship.

No pleasures last so well as good
fellowship and friendship.

To be on the receiving end of friendship, one must first learn to receive.

Friendship is picking up a telephone call from the other side of the world and feeling the distance melt away as the voice on the other end greets you.

One must not blame one's friends for one's own faults or actions. We are thrown into this world to be responsible for all that we do.

The roadmap to peace is friendship.

The supreme task for all of us is to take a step toward uniting the entire human race through the bond of friendship.

With friendship must come
the freedom to ask, to say,
to think, to do, and to be.

**Friendship is a cart—honesty
and commitment are its wheels.**

Friendship is a revelation.

Ambition has no friend.

Friends keep each other going.

Everyone deserves their friend's forgiveness. It is a bridge we must all cross many times in our lives, and it should never be broken.

Friendship is an entire philosophy.

A person must make new acquaintances on their advance through life or they will soon find themselves alone.

There is no good companion in this life who does not wish the same good to us as they do to themselves.

Friends are like twinned towns— they may look nothing alike, but their souls are in sympathy.

Friendship seeks to speak freely and act freely. There can be no friendship where there is no freedom.

Friends who show their love, and who value each other, set a fine example to the rest of the world.

Friendship's field is large and full of variety.

Friendship is not limited by the circumstances that bodies are confined to.

Friendship has at root an enduring nature.

Give two nations
opportunities
and they may
become friends.
Give two nations
weapons and
the chances are
they'll destroy
each other.

Everywhere two friends go, they soon discover that a poet or an analyst has been there before them.

If you make a wish for mankind, make it that all might live in friendlier times.

Friends must learn to be as patient with each other as nature is with each season.

Friendship survives the frostier times like the buds that blossom after the snows.

Friendship grants the right to be wrong, not the right to do wrong.

Having a friend to relate to inspires us to think over our own impulses, and to recognize in ourselves those things that give rise to behavior that we reproach in others.

In our limited lifespan on this earth nothing enhances our security so much as friendship.

Friendship represents freedom, because it lessens the extent of our wants and our dependence upon external things.

Suddenly we discover that we are doing favors for another and that they are doing favors for us. Friendship has been grafted in the orchard and both shall enjoy many harvests for years to come.

All tears have worth—a friend's tears are worth even more.

May our friendship provide us with virtue and courage to protect us from unexpected changes of fortune.

No kindness is too small to have great meaning to a friend.

A friendship governed by one person's will over the other invalidates the relationship.

To please friends requires only that we be honest and reliable.

No friend will disgrace the other.

Friends keep pace with each other, neither sets it.

Our friends never flatter. They praise only the qualities we have.

No one should ever play with human life.

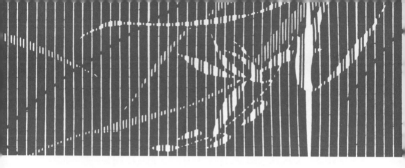

Friends do not offer each other happiness that they are unable to deliver.

Friendship is a kind word at just the right moment.

Let us be grateful to people who make us happy; they are the charming gardeners who make our souls blossom.

Marcel Proust

Why should we take care of our friendship? Imagine waking one day to discover the sun is no longer shining. That is what life would be like without your friends.

Why stop at other people? There is tremendous good in those who are the friends of all living things.

As we get older we come to realize that we are faced with simple choices:
To become a tyrant,
To become a slave,
Or to become a friend.

The world has no shortage of friends. What it lacks is the spirit of friendship.

God, if you are to bless me with anything, please let it be with a prudent friend.

Living in friendship is in itself a form of universal spirituality.

My friends are the source from which I may draw.

With friends there is no need to weigh our thoughts or measure our words.

Sit all of humankind in one place and there is one thing upon which they will all agree without hesitation—the importance of friendship and their desire for it.

Friendship is as broad as the horizon: to experience it we should develop a friendlier manner toward nature and all living things.

Nothing grows in a cold and hostile climate. Friendship requires warmth and friendliness if it is to take root.

The greatest test of character is friendship. It is one thing to prove one's loyalty to one's own family, but true loyalty to a friend is a mark of greatness.

Our hearts should be filled with compassion toward all our friends—we should fill their suffering hearts with love.

A little bit of light criticism never hurts, but one should never use a hammer to remove a fly from a friend's nose.

There is no height to be gained from pulling other people down. Friends are there to help pull each other up.

There are no strangers, only friends we haven't yet met.

When we can walk this earth with enthusiasm, we will gather friends like a polished mirror gathers dust.

Friends are always close to each other's hearts, even if they are on opposite sides of the globe.

One of the most reassuring feelings is knowing our friends will always be there to help us, should we need them.

In friendship we can get closer to accepting all the anxieties and difficulties of life.

One need not give up the world, or one's place in it to take to a life of friendship.

God was lonely so he invented humankind and offered them all his friendship.

There is only one universal language, and that is the language of the heart.

**Life without friendship
is a car without wheels.**

There is righteousness at
the heart of friendship.

There is harmony
in friendship.

The greatest wisdom of man is to know his own friends.

Friendship falls like raindrops on parched land.

Friendship is the bridge between earth and heaven.

Friendship embraces all
people, regardless of creed,
community, or language.

**In a friendly world there is nothing
to fear.
In a unfriendly world everyone
cowers in the shadows afraid.**

Happiness seems made
to be shared.

Jean Racine

The friendly heart gives and receives— it never takes.

When grief overtakes you, turn to your friends. But do not abandon them when joy returns to your life.

Friendship is that voice in your heart that tells you all is well, that you are being guarded and guided, and that you should feel no fear.

Tests of
Time

To me, fair friend, you never can be old.
For as you were when first your eye I eyed,
Such seems your beauty still.

William Shakespeare

A friend is more than a picture encased in a frame—each friend is a life encased in your heart.

One loyal friend is worth ten thousand relatives.

Euripides

Whatever our standing, king or peasant, the happiest of us are those who find peace in friendship.

If you have one true friend you have more than your share.
Thomas Fuller

The most exciting moments in our lives come to us when we are living for others.

There is no higher status to be achieved than rising to the position of being someone's best friend.

It is easy enough to be friendly to one's friends. But to befriend the one who regards himself as your enemy is the quintessence of true religion. The other is mere business.

Mahatma Gandhi

Skeptical men sit and wait for signs and miracles, while those with friendship in their hearts witness them every day.

Only solitary men know the full joys of friendship. Others have their family—but to a solitary and an exile his friends are everything.

Willa Cather

Friendship comes like fresh air to a drowning man.

I have three kinds of friends: those who love me, those who pay no attention to me, and those who detest me.

Sebastien-Roch Nicolas de Chamfort

**Friendship is instructive—
it offers both protection
and punishment.**

We few, we happy few,
  we band of brothers,
For he today that sheds
  his blood with me
Shall be my brother.
                    William Shakespeare

Be more prompt in going to a friend in adversity than in prosperity.

Chilo

Those with a friendly attitude toward life, this world, and the creatures in it do not weigh the status or caste of any individual before offering their friendship.

No man is so
perfect, so
necessary to his
friends, as to give
them no cause to
miss him less.
Jean de La Bruyère

**Friends listen
to each other and
in so doing hear
what they should
say to themselves.**

Real devotion to a friend should always be absolute and unconditional.

There is as much difference between the counsel that a friend giveth, and that a man giveth himself, as there is between the counsel of a friend and of a flatterer. For there is no such flatterer as is a man's self.

Sir Francis Bacon

Friendship is built upon constructive thoughts and positive actions.

Those who seek an entirely happy life will unwisely seek it in wealth and possessions, while the wiser will understand that the most valued possession one can ever have is friendship.

It is not helpful to help a friend by putting coins in his pockets when he has got holes in his pockets.

Douglas Hurd

She is such a good friend that she would throw all her acquaintances into the water for the pleasure of fishing them out again.

Charles Maurice de Talleyrand

Birth gives us life, but friendship gives us something to live for.

Make friends with the angels, who though invisible are always with you. Often invoke them, constantly praise them, and make good use of their help and assistance in all your temporal and spiritual affairs.

St. Francis de Sales

If friendship had a female name it would surely be Felicity.

Ceremony was but devised at first to set a gloss on faint deeds, hollow welcomes, recanting goodness, sorry ere 'Tis shown; but where there is true friendship, there needs none.

William Shakespeare

Our friends will always find the vein of gold that runs, un-mined, deep within us.

All colors are the friends of their neighbors and the lovers of their opposites.

Marc Chagall

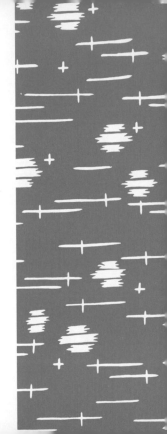

For character too is a process and an unfolding...among our valued friends is there not someone or other who is a little too self confident and disdainful; whose distinguished mind is a little spotted with commonness; who is a little pinched here and protuberant there with native prejudices; or whose better energies are liable to lapse down the wrong channel under the influence of transient solicitations?

George Eliot

To like and dislike the same things,
that is friendship.

**I don't like to commit myself about
heaven and hell—you see, I have
friends in both places.**

Mark Twain

Love is blind, but friendship
closes its eyes.

Fan the sinking flame of hilarity with the wing of friendship; and pass the rosy wine.

Charles Dickens

The feeling of friendship is like that of being comfortably filled with roast beef.

Samuel Johnson

The best compliment to a child or a friend is the feeling you give him that he has been set free to make his own inquiries, to come to conclusions that are right for him, whether or not they coincide with your own.

Alistair Cooke

Do everything that you do in this life in the spirit of friendship. For friendship is the seed, and the universe is the tree.

He who loses wealth loses much; he who loses a friend loses more.
Miguel de Cervantes

Who am I?
I am someone's friend.

It is wise to apply the oil of refined politeness to the mechanism of friendship.

Sidonie Gabrielle Colette

Be worthy of the esteem of your friends.

When a sinister person means to be your enemy, they always start by trying to become your friend.

William Blake

We can adopt, on the same terms, other men's knowledge—but not their friends.

Nothing is more dangerous than a friend without discretion; even a prudent enemy is preferable.

Jean de La Fontaine

Friendship demands not only a good nature, but also good sense.

Confidence is the bond of friendship.
Publilius Syrus

Have faith that your friend is with you at all times and in all places.

A Roman divorced from his wife, being highly blamed by his friends, who demanded, "Was she not chaste? Was she not fair? Was she not fruitful?" holding out his shoe, asked them whether it was not new and well made. "Yet," added he, "none of you can tell where it pinches me."

Plutarch

Your lost friends are not dead, but gone before, advanced a stage or two upon that road which you must travel in the steps they trod.

Aristophanes

Old friends are like old shoes— infinitely more comfortable.

If we want to gain a good opinion of ourselves we should turn to our friends for theirs.

No man is useless
while he has a friend.

Robert Louis Stevenson

There are two kinds of friends:
those who, when we are in trouble,
ask if there is anything they can do;
and those who just get on and do
something appropriate to help.

I no doubt deserved my enemies, but
I don't believe I deserved my friends.

Walt Whitman

I have always laid it down as a maxim that a man and a woman make far better friendships with the condition that they never have made or are to make love to each other.

Lord Byron

Life should not be measured by what
we get in return for our friendship, but
by what has happened because of it.

**Friendship is a delicate flower
you cannot gather its beauty by
plucking off all of its petals.**

A friend measures their
satisfaction by your own.

**Friendship is a tough nut to crack,
but the flesh is sweet.**

There is a great reality
beyond form and sound—
it is the friendship that
exists between two people.

**Friendship is a common belief in
the same fallacies, mountebanks,
and hobgoblins.**

H. L. Mencken

Friendship is expressed in compassionate acts and loving kindness.

Friendship is the perfection of love, and superior to love; it is love purified, exalted, proved by experience and a consent of minds.

Samuel Richardson

The most difficult thing to articulate properly, to make sound interesting, or have understood is describing your friendship with another to someone who does not know your friends.

In true friendship, in which I am expert, I give myself to my friend more than I draw him to me. I not only like doing him good better than having him do me good, but also would rather have him do good to himself than to me; he does me most good when he does himself good.

Michel de Montaigne

Love is a blazing, crackling, green-wood flame, as much smoke as flame; friendship, married friendship particularly, is a steady, intense, comfortable fire. Love, in courtship, is friendship in hope; in matrimony, friendship upon proof.

Samuel Richardson

You ask how many friends I have?
  Water and stone, bamboo and pine.
The moon rising over the eastern
  hill is a joyful comrade.
Besides these five companions,
  what other pleasure should I ask?

Yon Sun-do

Remove ego and desire
from your friendship and
you and your friend will
be left with peace.

What do we live for if not to make life less difficult for each other?

George Eliot

Friendships are coated in consoling words and deeds.

The wise are those of us who know who our true friends are.

Sometimes in our relationship to another human being the proper balance of friendship is restored when we put a few grains of impropriety onto our own side of the scale.

Friedrich Nietzsche

If everyone knew what they all said about each other, there would not be four friends left in the world.

Blaise Pascal

Friendship is the shadow of the evening, which strengthens with the setting sun of life.

Jean de La Fontaine

The bliss derived from friendship cannot be obtained from anything else.

It is a good thing to be rich, and a good thing to be strong, but it is a better thing to be beloved of many friends.

Euripides

Friendship is its own measure.

A mistress never is nor can be a friend.
While you agree, you are lovers; and
when it is over, anything but friends.

Lord Byron

**May you never live anyplace
where you have no friends, and
may the hand of a friend always
be near you.**

No distance of place or lapse of time can lessen the friendship of those who are thoroughly persuaded of each other's worth.

Robert Southey

Our friend's want is our desire.

Each friendship is infinite and incomparable—equal only to itself.

Friendship is its own witness.

Love is like the wild rose-briar;
Friendship like the holly-tree.
The holly is dark when the
    rose-briar blooms,
But which will bloom most
    constantly?

Emily Brontë

I am already kindly disposed towards you. My friendship it is not in my power to give: this is a gift which no man can make, it is not in our own power: a sound and healthy friendship is the growth of time and circumstance, it will spring up and thrive like a wildflower when these favour, and when they do not, it is in vain to look for it.

William Wordsworth

I wish that friendship should have feet, as well as eyes and eloquence. It must plant itself on the ground, before it vaults over the moon.

Ralph Waldo Emerson

The greatest sweetener of human life is friendship. To raise this to the highest pitch of enjoyment, is a secret which but few discover.

Joseph Addison

Friends should avoid boasting.
Be simple and sincere.

Fill each new day with friendliness.

Friendship is certainly the
finest balm for the pangs
of disappointed love.

Jane Austen

**Give friendship and you shall
receive friendship.**

In any long-term friendships things will change, people will change, circumstances will change. If you are able to flow with the changes, like water flowing through different pathways, you will prosper. If not, your friendship will flounder.

Solala Towler

Friends must realize that friendship is as much about obligations as it is about privileges.

A true friendship is as wise as it is tender. The parties to it yield implicitly to the guidance of their love, and know no other law nor kindness.

Henry David Thoreau

"Stay" is a charming word in a friend's vocabulary.

Louisa Mary Alcott

Learn to adapt and to adjust to accommodate your friends.

Truly great friends are hard to find, difficult to leave, and impossible to forget.

G. Randolf

No one has lived until they have discovered how to spend a perfectly unproductive summer's afternoon lazing about with a friend.

A day with a friend costs a day of your life—a cost well worth paying.

While others race about in search of retreats, friends simply retire into their friendship.

If we could read the secret history of our enemies, we should find in each man's life sorrow and suffering enough to disarm all hostility.

Henry Wadsworth Longfellow

Life is an exciting business, and most exciting when it is lived for others.

Helen Keller

There is no friend like silence.

Senecas de Beneficiis

When there is mutual goodwill and affection and an accord in all things, friendship has taken root.

When I play with my cat, how do I know that she is not passing time with me rather than I with her?

Michel de Montaigne

The moments when you have really lived will have been the moments when you did things in a spirit of friendship.

This above all: to
thine own self be true,
And it must follow, as
the night the day,
Thou canst not then
be false to any man.

William Shakespeare

We can only be wise alone if we occasionally balance it by going a bit wild with a friend.

A good marriage is based on the talent for friendship.
Friedrich Nietzsche

It isn't true friendship until we are prepared and able to defend our friends against our own influence.

Do not wish that your benefactor may need to be repaid by you, but only that you may be able to repay him, if he needs it.

Few things tend more to alienate friendship than a want of punctuality in our engagements. I have known the breach of a promise to dine or sup to break up more than one intimacy.

William Hazlitt

The time you enjoy wasting with your friends is not wasted time.

Secrecy is the chastity of friendship.
Jeremy Taylor

Time makes
friendship stronger,
but love weaker
　　　Jean de La Bruyère

The most accessible
pleasure is talking with good
friends. It is the best value
communication that exists.

If we would build on a sure foundation in friendship, we must love friends for their sake rather than for our own.

Charlotte Brontë

Ask any person how many friends they think they have and they will never be able to be certain.

The rule of friendship means there should be mutual sympathy between them, each supplying what the other lacks and trying to benefit the other, always using friendly and sincere words.

Buddha

In every mess I find a friend.

Charles Dibdin

The greatest secrets kept are the mistakes and imperfections that are within us, and which are pointed out to us by our friends.

The celebratory flame of prosperity burns twice as brightly in the company of a friend.

Friendship is like archeology—it unearths our spirit, and sets it free once more for all to gaze at.

Mighty proud I am that I am able to have a spare bed for my friends.

Samuel Pepys

The finest ornaments to adorn anybody's house would have to be the friends who frequent it.

The language of friendship is not words but meanings.

Henry David Thoreau

Don't walk in front of me, I may not follow. Don't walk behind me, I may not lead. Walk beside me and be my friend.

Albert Camus

Who Needs
Enemies?

Make friends with your enemies and thereby destroy the latter.

Those who live in and near the river should make every effort to befriend the crocodiles.

Beware of those who gossip—for whoever gossips to you, will eventually gossip about you.

Nothing thaws a cold, bitter heart like the warmth of true friendship.

Adversity is the only reliable scale to use to discover the balance of friendship.

The most injurious blow one could wield to a friend is one that is self-inflicted.

The difference between us and the animal kingdom is that the lion is never friendly toward the lamb before it devours it.

When a person betrays their friends, in truth, what they are betraying is their very own conscience.

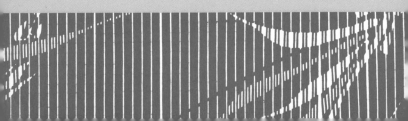

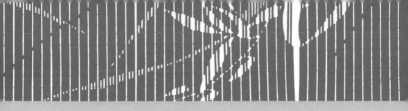

Many an injurious inferno
has been fanned to life from
the last dying embers of an
extinguished friendship.

**We all are born with the choice:
to either build ourselves a
fortress against life or to fortify
life with excellent friendships.**

Why does man insist upon embarking on a path to success that is paved with the destruction of his family, his beliefs, and his friends?

Don't let success cloud your vision. Having faithful friends is not the same as having people around you who are paid to kiss your feet.

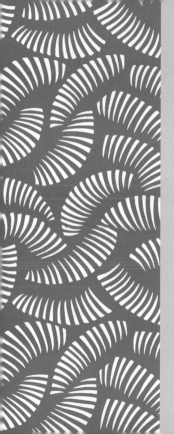

When enemies offer their hands, offer yours back in a spirit of friendship.

I admire those people who stick up for their friends even in their absence.

It is not friendship to turn acquaintances into intimate friends the moment they achieve success.

Some feel themselves brave enough to go through life friendless, but it is one thing to talk of bulls and quite another to be in the bullring.

If you are ready to believe in all who say "Trust me," then you are easy to deceive.

A friendship that has no trust is like seeking shelter from the rain under a leaky roof.

One should never lie to a friend: if we are determined to experiment with truth, then we should do so with our own lives, not the lives of those closest to us.

Where there is injustice in this world, you will also find a global friendship born out of those people linked by their opposition to it.

When you say: "you are my friend," mean it.

The worst enemy you can ever have is the one who was once your best friend.

Friendship takes no ill where no ill was meant.

Every tyrant's heart is poisoned by the belief that he cannot trust any of his friends.

The friend you feel compelled to buy will never be worth the sum you paid.

One cannot create a friendship through falsehood.

Is it really so hard to die for a friend? Not as hard as one would imagine when it comes right down to it. No, the hardest thing in life is finding a friend worth dying for.

When the words of your enemies are ringing in your head, find peace by meditating on the silence of your friend.

Who is mad enough to choose to perish as enemies when it is perfectly possible to live together as friends?

Beware the friends who only like you because they cannot get the friends they would rather have.

Do not bring down all your might upon your enemy, for he may one day become your friend.

**Instead of loving your enemies,
treat your friends a little better.**

Edgar Watson Howe

The most difficult thing to
repair is your word when
you have broken it.

**People, over time, become too
attached to material things to pry
themselves away for long enough
to grow attached to other people.**

Friends are like the strings on a violin: a joy when they are in harmony, but overwind them and they're likely to snap.

Breaking promises weakens the ties of friendship.

No one can force
another to become their
friend against their will.

Do not imagine you
can purchase friends by
offering gifts, you will soon
discover that when the gifts
cease, so will their love.

Of course it is awful to be deceived by a friend, but it is even worse to go through life distrusting one's friends.

Take strides to make friends with yourself—only then will you rid yourself of your own worst enemy.

It isn't friendship if all the time you are together each is thinking that the other could cut their throat while they're sleeping.

What is there to compare friendship to if one has never had friends?

It is always a race as to who will be the first to find your faults— your friend or your foe.

Treacherous conduct cannot be hidden for long from those close to us.

Beware those who have ways of discovering the interior of another, yet are able to hide their own.
They seek only gain.

Friends and enemies have the same language.

Turning to your friends only in times of trouble is like the sinner who believes in God only when he has a fever.

There is no forgiveness for those who lead their friends into sorrow.

True friendship never places one in the position of having to choose between right and wrong.

It is easier to forgive an enemy than to forgive a friend.

William Blake

False friends are like thieves—they take all and give nothing back.

True friendship is discovered when your love affair breaks up. Friends will rally to one side or the other, and will develop a sudden aversion to match your own for your former partner.

We do not get the friends we desire,
we get the friends that we deserve.

**Have friendship, and you will find
you can brave any kind of calamity
that may ensue.**

Anger in friendship
is derived from love.

There is no such thing as strangers, only friends who have not yet decided whether to take you up on your friendship.

Friendship offers order to mankind, and with it the opportunity for worldwide peace.

Friendship is unsinkable.

When friendship begins to fail who can one blame but oneself? The gardener doesn't blame his flowers or his fruit when crops fail, he looks to his own actions and remedies the problem. So must we.

Never become friends to gain money. It is cheaper by far to borrow it from a bank.

If we look for the devil in a friend he will surely appear.

Beware those who pretend at friendship for they are worse than any foe.

There is nothing quite as pathetic as watching a man embarked on the impossible mission of attempting to win friends by trying to get them interested in him. Were he simply to turn his attention and his own interest toward them he would succeed.

There are plenty who would be your friends—true, honest friends, however, are few on the ground.

Before borrowing money
from a friend, first decide
which of the two you
need most.

**Reveal not every secret you have
to a friend, for how can you tell
but that friend may hereafter
become an enemy. And bring not
all mischief you are able to upon
an enemy, for he may one day
become your friend.**

Saadi

When choosing friends, take care to select only those who act conscientiously toward themselves. For only if they do, can you depend upon them to act conscientiously toward you.

If you seek a peaceful life always speak well of your friends, and say nothing of your enemies.

The most poisonous thing known to friendship is doubt.

Rats desert a sinking friendship.

A hollow friend is as much
good as a leaking canoe.

Do not repay friendship with hurt.

Necessity never made
a good friendship.

False friends are nothing more than shadows. They choose to walk through life with us while the sun shines, but in our dark moments they disappear from sight.

Avoid those who would come to disturb or destroy your friendship.

We all, thank God, have the potential to be fooled by love and duped by friendship. The alternative would be to despise this world and all in it.

If you just want a friend who will do all as you do: cry because you cry, laugh because you laugh, jump because you jump, it would be better to spend your life looking at your own reflection in the garden pond.

Do not protect yourself with a fence, but rather with your friends.

**What is a friendly community?
A small group of caring, thoughtful, committed citizens—who together can change the world.**

When the friend is ready the friend appears.

It is easier to visit friends than to have them live with you under the same roof.

None of us is so rich that we can afford to throw away a friend.

It is better in times of need to have a friend rather than money.

Seek a friend who is without a single fault and you will spend your entire life friendless.

Better to make a friend
Than fear an enemy.

**Happiness is arriving at a point in
life where there is nothing to fear
from those around you.**

Be suspicious of an enemy's report of
what a friend has said or done. They
may unconsciously be telling the truth.

A friend likes
you despite your
achievements.

**Anyone has the potential to
become our friend if we are
prepared to close an eye.**

There are no rules to friendship. It crosses all divides, rivers, tribes, steeples, sexes, calendars, clocks, and colors.

Nothing can sting quite so painfully as the bitterly cold words of a friend.

Pat your friend on the back—
but never with a hatchet.

**A friendship bought with money
is worse than no friendship at all.**

He who doesn't
have friendship
doubts friendship.

Short on friends. Short on brains.

No matter the circumstances, when a friend cries out to you for help, you will always find in you that extra bit of strength to do so.

We are defined by our friends, and also our enemies.

Each new friend brings with them mutual enemies.

One should never close one's heart and mind off to the possibility of friendship.

Before envying anyone else's friendship, examine how happy they actually are in it.

**Never underestimate
the importance of your
friendship to others.**

The human race has one really
effective weapon—friendship.

**A friend believes in you even when
the rest of the world does not.**

Hostility cannot undo a knot
tied by friendship.

No true friend would ever seek to belittle your ambitions.

Better a friend who is filled with doubts than one who is fanatically certain of everything.

You know a person is your friend when you begin to feel guilty for their misdeeds.

Never condemn the judgment of a friend simply because it differs from your own. Consider that both of you may be wrong.

You know your friendship's in trouble when you invite your friends for dinner and then find yourself counting the cutlery after they've gone.

If you keep a green bough in your heart, eventually a singing bird will come.

Never envy your friends. Envy eats up everything good in a friendship as a fire devours an entire forest.

Each friend is sweet and each friend is sour.

Before judging the actions of a friend, consider first their intentions.

Beware a friend who places his arm around the shoulder of your enemy.

Beware the enemy who places his arm around your shoulder.

Beware your reaction to your friend when your enemy places his arm around his shoulder.

We can all alter our lives simply and immediately by altering the attitude of our minds. Implant a friendly attitude and friendship will surely follow.

Life's
Lessons

What is more spiritually inspiring than the discovery that someone else believes in you so much that they are willing to place their trust in you?

Friendship is the godmother of invention.

Spend the day with friendship in your heart.

A friendship is built out of
caring, sharing, and giving.
It is something very special
that just happens to us one
fine day and remains with us
for the rest of our lives.

We love our friends not only
for being themselves, but also
for what we are when we are
with them.

First a person accepts the friendship of another and then gives friendship back to that other—until friendship takes over them both.

None of us are taught how to live our lives, and risking it alone can mean wasting a life. Friendship helps us to distinguish what things in life are worth living through.

Friends go through life together most agreeably, each having firm confidence in the other as the foundation for their own life.

There is a difference between someone stretching out their hand in friendship, and someone stretching out their hand in want of friendship.

People are rarely themselves. We feel compelled to put up fronts to deal with the world and take them down only in the midst of our closest companions.

When there are two friends in your life, seek advice from the one who is able to move you to tears before the one who is able to make you laugh.

The beginning of wisdom is to call things by their right names. A friend is a friend.

When we make the simple decision to bring the love of friendship into our lives, from that very instant of committing ourselves, providence comes in to play.

Relationships are a way of life—and friendship puts the life into living.

I like my friends, and my friends like me. We like all the disputes and all the agreements—and everything, it seems, leads only to us liking each other even more.

You ask me what I am worth? It can only be measured in friendships.

May we give ourselves
to friendship.

Going through life
with a friend is a
true education.

Lasting friendships are like
Rome—they cannot be built
in a day, but a good day is a
good place to start.

One way of looking at friendship is this: we cannot choose our friends, they are self-elected. Once they have elected to be our friends, then we can be choosy.

We all have one person who we crown as our best friend, but one should also look to oneself—and make oneself one's best friend too.

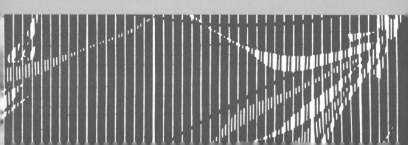

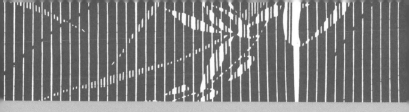

Each moment should be made
    meaningful in our lives
Each day, and each one of our
    friends, should have
    meaning to us
And even though things pass
Their meaning remains with us
    always.

A garden is a good friend—one can visit any time one likes.

Some of the most lasting and meaningful relationships are friendships forged between two people who once despised each other, and found good reason not to.

Mothers and their children have something that goes beyond love. It is a deep friendship that continues to develop as they raise each other in their new roles as mother and child.

A friend is someone who understands your past, believes in your future, and accepts you today just the way you are.

Proverbs 27:17

The criticism that is the most difficult to take, yet should be valued most, is that which comes from our closest friend— for it is probably the most honest criticism we shall ever hear.

Some friends are as alike as chalk and cheese, and others like and dislike the very same things—two fundamentally different friendships, yet both with the potential to last.

Friendship is not something to be flaunted in public. A true friend will not seek to benefit from glamor or intrigue, or from boasting about his friend's position in society.

The feeling of friendship permeates every fiber of our being.

The true meaning of life is to plant friendship and enjoy the shade. Plant a tree in the spirit of friendship—you may not benefit from its shade yourself, but someone in the future will.

Peace, liberty, brotherhood, prosperity, and justice—these are all attributes of friendship and they are freely available to all of us with friendship in our hearts.

We give, on average, almost one-third of our lives up for sleep, and around half of our waking hours to work. The wise among us also give over a quarter of our time to being in the company of friends—and in doing so, our lives becomes a veritable feast and a cause for celebration.

If you
close your
door to
a friend
where
else can
they go?

Walking along through life
in friendship is a journey
steeped in wonder.

**The path to friendship cannot be
taught by others. Friends will find
each other—walk in nothingness
and seek nothing, and they will come.**

What every government should come to know is that most people, if forced to choose, would elect to betray their country before they would betray their friend.

In the bright eyes of someone else's friendship, we can see the reflection of our own.

Pure friendship is boundless and infinite. Once we have gained this understanding there is nothing more to try to understand; it is better simply to relax and enjoy it.

In a life filled with friendship, there is a heart filled with gladness.

If there is one good reason as to why we have been placed upon this earth, it must be for the sake of friendship— for where there is friendship there is growth.

One should never attempt to change the appearance of one's friends. Better to accept them as they are and alter your own way of looking at them.

Bliss is found in the joy of a friend.

Friendship is its own authority.

Everything in life, it seems, is managed by order, method, and discipline—except, thank goodness, for friendship.

Never attempt to trap or encage a friend. To do so would result in capturing only their reflection.

Friends will not hesitate to take on each other's troubles.

The proof of a friend's sincerity is that they pay no heed to that which is not their business.

There is no room for generalization when it comes to a friendship. It is one of the most important investments any person will ever make. Get it right and reap the dividends.

No need to weigh your thoughts—your friends will weigh them for you.

How might we know the reality of our friendship? If we can derive pleasure from the good we perform and grieve for any bad acts we may have committed, then we are a true friend.

Start the day with
thoughts of a friend.

End the day with a friend.

Friendship lights
the way.

Friendship asks only this: that we be what we profess to be, that we speak what we intend to do, and that we honestly relate our experiences.

Whatever you speak— your friends hear.

Whatever you do— your friends witness.

Friendliness must always blossom into a friendship.

Friendship is happiness
Happiness is awareness
Awareness is friendship.

Do not live life merely for food, entertainment, frivolity, ease, envy, and pride. Live it for the peace, joy, and calm that comes through being someone's friend.

Our life here is as temporary as each floating cloud, our friendships go on despite us.

If one can love one's self and others, then this is the truest form of universal friendship.

Everything apart from friendship yields only momentary pleasures.

Friendship is love.
Live in Love.

Friendship is truth.
Live in Truth.

Friendship is bliss.
Live in Bliss.

Do not approach friendship by overturning friends' opinions and observations, but contribute to them and build upon them. Together friends can reach heights neither alone would have imagined possible.

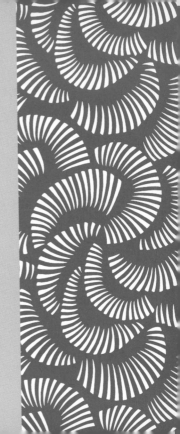

Friendship is based
upon pure thoughts
and a pure heart,
true devotion and
outstretched arms.

Friendship is the
mutual offering of
hearts to one another.

When you need
reassurance, close
your eyes and your
friend will be there.

435

Nothing but heaven itself is better than a friend who is really a friend.

Plautus

We cannot always assure the future of our friends; we have a better chance of assuring our future if we remember who our friends are.

Henry Kissinger

One can achieve far more by practicing friendship than by talking about it.

Can there be anything greater than earning the love, respect, and devotion of another person?

A friend wipes away our tears of grief and replaces them with tears of joy.

**Let go of your burdens and
open your heart so that you
may fill it, and your arms, with
precious friendship.**

Friendship is the free
expression of people's
unshakeable love for each
other—love that is pure,
noble, and free from desire
for personal gain.

Fate chooses your relations, you choose your friends.
Jacques Delille

Friendliness is goodness.

Beauty is a friend.

439

**Truth, belief, peace, and love
are the pillars on which the
mansion of friendship is built.**

We are not in search of
friendship, we are the friend
that someone else will find.

**Friendship comes like moonlight
on the darkest night.**

Being a good friend to another can
be a spiritual practice on its own.

Solala Towler

Consider
the universal
implications
of friendship
and adopt
the world as
your country,
for all the
people of
this world
are made
for helping
each other.

Friends seem always to be aware of our suffering, and how we can best escape it.

My friends are there at the drop of a hat.

All the joy we crave is within us from birth. It takes friendship to set it free.

There is great beauty in the character of friendship.

My friends are part of the sum total of my life.

Life without friendship is like swimming without water.

A friend's words are taken to heart—like matches to candles they illuminate our life.

Nourish your friends and revere them. They are everything that is good in your life.

Friendship is the swiftest path to contentment—and there is no greater provider of happiness than that.

Friendship teaches us to be less judgmental toward others. This leaves us time to enjoy and love them.

Being a friendlier person is its own reward. Add to it peace of mind, inner joy and the friendliness people will show you in return, and you'll wonder why you were ever unfriendly before.

Recline in the comfort of your friendship.

A friend asks for only two things— our friendship and our love.

Wholesome happiness arises from the fullness of friendship.

Everything that exists externally to us has the potential to fail us. Friendship dwells within and can always be relied upon.

Let your yearning be for wisdom, virtue, and good thoughts—this is the path to the good life.

Difficulties are created to help us sift the sincere devoted friends from the rest.

Now more than ever before, perhaps, the world is in need of friendship. It begins within ourselves and stretches to the four corners of the globe, and it is the only way the world will survive this century— so start making friends today.

Friendship must emanate from the heart, for that is where it resides— next to peace, trust, and faith.

To become eligible for friendship, one must first be capable of being loved.

Love is truly a pleasure for a season or two, but true friendship lasts for ever.

Friendship has a way of making everything a bit more noble.

Friends know that happiness will not come from simply trying to satisfy each other's vanity.

When we give out love and respect to those around us that is what we will receive in return.

Hua Ching Ni

The honor of a friendship is in its mutual independence.

Passion is full of stormy delights, but friendship brims over with calm pleasure.

All friendship is desirable in itself.

Friends would never fish for flattery using the bait of self-criticism.

Life is an intricate operation— friendship is the anesthetic.

Friendship is like a dragonfly to a pond. The pond does not chase the insect, but lies still until it alights upon the water.

Friendship is an understanding between two people, which brings them both peace.

One who walks in another's tracks leaves no footprints. Friendship's footprints are side by side.

Nothing is more entire and without reserve, more zealous, contented, affectionate, or sincere than the constancy of friendship.

The single most important acquisition for a happy life is friendship.

Knowledge remains isolated and barren until it is accompanied by love and trust in our friends.

Enter friendship with no expectation of return. In the long run a friend is worth more than a lover.

Friendship is an invitation to just be ourselves.

Our friend is our selected relation. The bond goes beyond blood ties — nearer to that territory we refer to as sacred.

Friendship is the most solid form known to mankind.

Friendship is the golden light that shines not upon finite reality, but upon the infinite possibility of our lives.

If you can get past our hard outer shell, deep inside each of us is the pearl of friendship.

Seen through the eyes of our friendship, all things and all beings can become beautiful.

Whatever happens in our lives, we will never run out of people to love.

One should never feel one's desire for friendship as something silly— don't we all long to be understood by others?

A true friend embosoms freely,
advises justly, assists readily,
adventures boldly, takes all patiently,
defends courageously, and
continues a friend unchangeably.

William Penn

**Friends help each other to
become that which each is
capable of being.**

The best time to make friends is well before you need them.

The golden key of selflessness opens the lock which keeps the door to friendship shut.

When troubles come, look beyond the dark clouds to the blue skies of friendship.

Henceforth I call
you not servants;
for the servant
knoweth not what
his lord doeth:
but I have called
you friends; for all
things that I have
heard of my Father
I have made known
unto you.

John 15:15

May we each and every one of us find freedom, peace, and friendship.

Shantih shantih shantih.

Published by MQ Publications Limited
12 The Ivories, 6–8 Northampton Street
London N1 2HY
email: mqp@mqpublications.com
website: www.mqpublications.com

Copyright © 2003 MQ Publications Limited
Text © 2003 David Baird

Design concept: Broadbase
Design: Philippa Jarvis

ISBN: 1-84072-559-1

1 0 9 8 7 6 5 4 3 2

Printed and bound in China

When we despise ourselves we hurt our friends.

Friendship cannot be planned.

The sufferings of a friend are nothing compared to the sufferings of some people at the success of their friends.

Even the wisest person alive would be a fool to avoid friendship.

A few close friends is a blessing, but to be the friend of the masses can be a curse.

The more we know a friend, the more we are able to forgive.

Many a friend is harmed by their best friend's best intentions.

Self-esteem must always be taken into consideration within a friendship.

Honor the memory of friends.

Success wins false friends.

Friendship is priceless.

A dying friend seeks no pity, but pities those friends who will survive him.

If you wish for perfect friends, best look for them among angels.

We all need to grow, our friends see us change, and we watch our friends change. But that doesn't mean we have to change friends.

Our friends are an instant indicator of change within ourselves.

A true friend is someone who is there for you even when they'd planned to be somewhere else.

Each of us is born to take different paths through life, but when we have friendship it doesn't matter where we go—there is always a little bit of our friend with us, and a little bit of us with them.

Friendship is like a recorded symphony— we may press the pause button from time to time, but release it and it's just as good as it was before.

A good long talk with a friend can cure almost anything.

If personal pleasure is the ultimate goal of all our actions then our lives would include others only as a means to our own selfish gratifications.

Friends have forgiving natures, especially when it comes to our mistakes.

An understanding friend is often the very best therapy.

You may give up on yourself, but your friend will never give up on you.

Don't be dismayed at good-byes.
A farewell is necessary before you
can meet again. And meeting
again, after moments or lifetimes,
is certain for those who are friends.

Richard Bach

Even after years have passed, there is never any time to be made up when two close friends reunite.

It is usually clear what things are good for a friendship, and what things are hurtful to it—those things which we are uncertain about are best avoided.

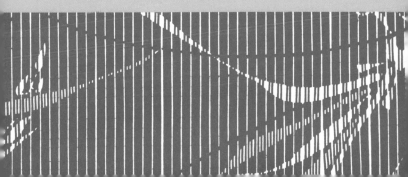

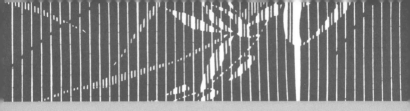

A friend is
impossible to forget.

**The advice of our friends
may be offered lovingly,
but we are not compelled
to follow it blindly.**

One should always take care never to forsake old friends.

The same wind that blows two vessels together could just as easily blow them away from each other.

One who is prepared to wound or offend a friend for their own good displays a healthy love for them.